Juneteenth

Buddy BOOKS
Holidays

ABDO
Publishing Company

A Buddy Book
by
Julie Murray

VISIT US AT
www.abdopublishing.com

Published by ABDO Publishing Company, 8000 West 78th Street, Edina, Minnesota 55439.

Printed in the United States of America, North Mankato, Minnesota.
052011
092011

 PRINTED ON RECYCLED PAPER

Coordinating Series Editor: Rochelle Baltzer
Editor: Sarah Tieck
Contributing Editors: Megan M. Gunderson, BreAnn Rumsch, Marcia Zappa
Graphic Design: Denise Esner
Cover Photograph: *Alamy*: ©Richard Levine.
Interior Photographs/Illustrations: *Alamy*: David R. Frazier Photolibrary, Inc. (p. 11),
     Jeff Greenberg (p. 5), A.T. Willett (p. 17); *AP Photo*: AP Photo/June 1965 (p. 22),
     PRNewsFoto/Greater Philadelphia Tourism Marketing Corporation, George Widman
     Photography (p. 21); *Getty Images*: The Bridgeman Art Library (p. 7), David Paul Morris
     (pp. 15, 17); *Library of Congress*: Brady National Photographic Art Gallery
     (Washington, D.C.) (p. 9); North Wind Picture Archives (p. 8); *PhotoEdit*: Tom Carter
     (p. 13), Bob Daemmrich (p. 5); *Shutterstock*: April Turner (p. 19).

Library of Congress Cataloging-in-Publication Data

Murray, Julie, 1969-
  Juneteenth / Julie Murray.
     p. cm. -- (Holidays)
  ISBN 978-1-61783-039-6
  1. Juneteenth--Juvenile literature. 2. Slaves--Emancipation--Texas--Juvenile literature. 3. African Americans--Texas--Galveston--History--Juvenile literature. 4. African Americans--Anniversaries, etc.--Juvenile literature. 5. African Americans--Social life and customs--Juvenile literature. 6. Slaves--Emancipation--United States--Juvenile literature. I. Title.
  E185.93.T4M86 2012
  394.263--dc22
                                            2011002290

Table of Contents

What Is Juneteenth?

Juneteenth happens every year on June 19. It is a holiday that honors the end of **slavery** in the United States.

On Juneteenth, people **celebrate** African-American **culture** and history. They hold parades and picnics. Many pray or attend church. People tell stories and share food. They also sing and play games.

The name *Juneteenth* comes from this holiday's date. People shortened June nineteenth to "Juneteenth."

Let Freedom Ring

Before the **American Civil War**, many African Americans were **slaves** in the United States. They were often bought in **auctions**. Their owners made them work hard. Many owners beat or hurt slaves.

At auctions, slave family members could be bought by different owners. Many families were separated.

The United States was split on the subject of **slavery**. It was one of the main causes of the **American Civil War**.

During the war, many African Americans were freed from slavery. But, slaves in Texas did not know this until after the war ended.

During the American Civil War, the Northern states were called the Union. The Southern states were called the Confederacy.

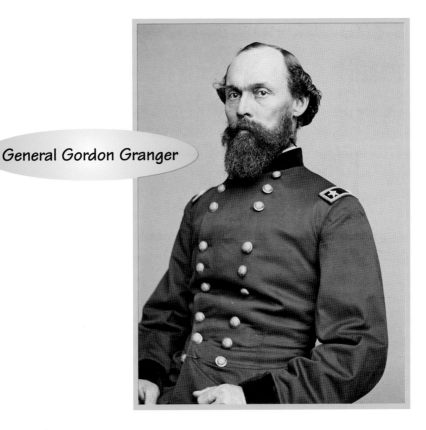

General Gordon Granger

On June 19, 1865, Northern troops came to Galveston, Texas. General Gordon Granger told the **slaves** there they were free. Some prayed, feasted, and danced to **celebrate**! They were the last slaves to be freed.

A Holiday Is Born

After 1865, people kept **celebrating** the end of **slavery** on June 19. The first Juneteenth celebrations were held in Texas. Over the years, people began holding events around the country.

Juneteenth first became a state holiday in Texas in 1980. Today, Juneteenth is observed in many places across the United States. It is the oldest celebration honoring the end of slavery.

Texas state representative Al Edwards helped Juneteenth become a recognized holiday in his state. A statue of him stands in Galveston.

Pass It On

Many **slaves** lived and worked on large farms called plantations. They often worked outside, picking cotton or other crops. Most were not allowed to learn to read. So, they used art and storytelling to share information.

On Juneteenth, African Americans remember their history. Some tell stories about their past through songs, plays, or art.

One way African Americans share their history on Juneteenth is by giving speeches. Sometimes, speakers dress up as historical figures.

A New Life

Slaves worked very hard. They were not fed well. And, they often wore rags or dirty clothes to work in the fields.

On Juneteenth, African Americans enjoy things slaves couldn't. Some wear new clothes. Others cook a feast. They have special foods such as corn bread, sweet potatoes, and pecan pie.

On Juneteenth, many people eat barbecue and other traditional Southern foods.

Games and other fun activities take place at Juneteenth events. People play baseball and have cakewalks. There are rodeos and parades, too.

Music is another important part of Juneteenth. On plantations, **slaves** sang songs to help with their work. Music was also used for worship and for fun. Today, music is an important part of African-American **culture**.

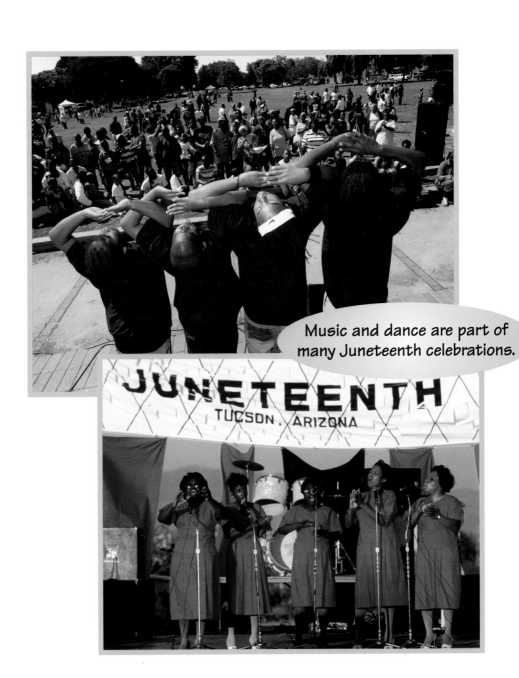

Music and dance are part of many Juneteenth celebrations.

Blood Red

The color red is an important part of Juneteenth. It stands for the blood of **slaves** and those who fought for their freedom.

For Juneteenth, people often decorate with red banners. They may fly the Juneteenth flag, which has red in it. And, they eat red foods at events.

Red soda is a traditional Juneteenth drink.

The Juneteenth flag uses the same colors as the American flag. The star in the middle represents Texas.

Juneteenth Today

Today on Juneteenth, African Americans remember their **heritage**. They honor their accomplishments and their freedom.

Juneteenth is **celebrated** in many places across the United States. Some events are simple and small. Others are large events at public buildings and parks. All celebrations help people remember how June 19, 1865, changed lives.

The African American Museum in
Philadelphia, Pennsylvania, honors
African-American history.

Freedom and Equality

Even though **slavery** ended in the 1860s, life was still hard for African Americans. Many people said that those with skin of a different color were not equal. They often treated African Americans badly or unfairly.

African Americans have fought for equality for more than 100 years. In the 1950s and the 1960s, this fight became known as the civil rights movement. Over time, Juneteenth has become a **symbol** of this fight, too.

Martin Luther King Jr. was an important civil rights leader.

Important Words

American Civil War the war between the Northern and Southern states from 1861 to 1865.

auction (AWK-shuhn) a public sale at which something is sold to the person who offers to pay the most money.

celebrate to observe a holiday with special events. These events are known as celebrations.

culture the arts, beliefs, and ways of life of a group of people.

heritage a tradition or practice that is handed down from the past.

slaves people bought and sold as property. Slavery is the act of owning slaves.

symbol (SIHM-buhl) an object or mark that stands for an idea.

Web Sites

To learn more about Juneteenth,
visit ABDO Publishing Company online. Web sites about Juneteenth are featured on our Book Links page. These links are routinely monitored and updated to provide the most current information available.

www.abdopublishing.com

Index